# HOW TO SUCCEED
# AT
# JOB INTERVIEWS
# THE EASYWAY

# HOW TO SUCCEED
# AT
# JOB INTERVIEWS
# THE EASYWAY

## Jeanette Benisti

Editor: Roger Sproston

Easyway Guides

Easyway Guides


© Straightforward Co Ltd 2023

978-1-80236-230-5


Printed by  4Edge www.4edge.co.uk


Cover design by BW Studio Derby

# Contents

\*\*\*\*

# Introduction

This latest edition of *How to Succeed at Job Interviews-The Easyway*, updated to 2023, is a comprehensive introduction to gaining the skills necessary to carry yourself through a job interview and to ensuring that you are at least in with a fighting chance of landing the job that you want.

As we all know, the last few years have changed the job market enormously. Since Brexit, then the pandemic, which brought in the phenomenon of working from home and now with the current cost of living crisis, the pattern of recruiting has changed.

It is true to say that at the current time there is a labour shortage and jobs are more readily available. However, the need to hone up on your interview skills, and be in with a fighting chance of getting a job, is very important.

Remote interviewing has been on the rise and is still prevalent. Job-seeking candidates are being advised to practice ahead of a remote interview. This is because interviewing remotely and interviewing in person are two completely different experiences,

This book is thorough, beginning with a look at what employers want when they place an advert and also how to interpret job advertisements. The media used by prospective employers is also examined. The interview process is discussed, together with the actual process of planning, research and development that is essential prior to attending a job interview.

The nature of tests, which often crop up in an interview situation, and the different variety of tests that may have to be undergone, is discussed at length, as is the process of making a presentation. Many jobs will require some sort of presentation and the skills necessary to present with confidence are outlined.

Included in this edition is a chapter (8) on telephone and Zoom/ Skype interviews. We also mention interview by video which is also used frequently. The format of these interviews is slightly different to the conventional interview and the skills needed to handle these types of interviews are also slightly different. Finally, if you are attending a conventional face-to-face interview, what to expect, plus likely interview questions and model answers is set out clearly and concisely.

How to Succeed at Job Interviews the Easyway is perhaps the most comprehensive book on the market today. It deals with all aspects of job applications and interviews, and is designed to instil confidence in the reader, whatever your position, whether you are new to the job market or looking to move jobs.

A sample CV and covering letters is set out in the index along with useful tips on filling in an application form.

****

# INTERPRETING JOB ADVERTS

# Chapter 1

# Employer's Requirements-Advertisements and What Employers Look for in a Candidate

---

**Understanding adverts**

Understanding the job advertisement is the key to putting together an application form or CV. Your application form/CV needs to be formulated with that specific job in mind and it is of fundamental importance that you are able to interpret and analyze the advertisement and make correct deductions. If you do not, then you will miss the point and you may not progress to the next stage.

**How the job is described**

All advertisements will tell the reader the name, location and business of the company. These will be put across in a positive way. Next will come the job description. Take time to think about how the job is described. This will enable you to get a real idea of what the company is after. Look to see whether you will be working alone or in a team. This is very important, particularly when emphasizing skills and experience on your application/CV. The company will describe what they do, what they require, then go on to outline qualifications and experience required. Obviously, this is one of the most important areas of the advertisement and should be read with care and clearly understood. In some cases, qualifications and experience required will be clearly stated. However, in other cases they won't and it will be up to you to infer these from the advert, based on your knowledge of the job.

## Salary

The salary attached to a job can be misleading as in many cases the actual salary to be offered is not quoted. Statements such as "attractive salary package" or "salary commensurate with age and experience" are employed. The rule here is that if a salary is very attractive it will be quoted. Look at what is said about the salary. The word "circa" may mean 'around' but quite often read by potential applicants as a minimum.

Many advertisements, particularly for posts in the public sector, give salary ranges. This shows interested applicants what their potential would be as well as the starting salary. Most organizations will negotiate the starting salary after they have made a decision to employ someone.

## Company description and philosophy

Look at what the company has to say for itself. This usually tells you how it wants to perceive itself rather than how others see it. The company may state that it is expanding, or might give that impression by advertising for a number of positions. You might get an idea of the possible promotion prospects from the advertisement. Be wary if there is a lack of company description. This does not always mean that there is a problem, the company may be huge and well known, therefore an in-depth description is not necessary. However, there may well be a flip side and the company may have something to hide, such as concealing recruitment information from other staff. On company philosophy, look for equal opportunity's statements etc. These vary enormously, with the public sector generally leading the way. You also need to consider how important the existence of an equal opportunities statement is for you.

## Media used to advertise position

The medium used to advertise the post can tell you a lot. If an advertisement is in a national paper, then it usually means that the employer has decided that they will spend more money in order to cast their net wider, i.e., nationally instead of locally. Some companies use agencies. This means that they have chosen to have the screening done by another party. In this case, it will be your job to convince the agency that they should introduce you to the company. Sometimes, the agency carries out initial interviews and only submits the short list to their client.

You may want to consider making your application more general if the agency handles many jobs in the industry in which you work. Think about the reasons why the organizations use agencies. Do they want specialists for whom that agency is known? Do they not have much expertise in that area themselves?

This can be true when companies are seeking personnel at the top of a department, where there is nobody above with the kind of knowledge required to recruit that person.

Good advertisements are not only the right size but are also the right shape too. They have usually been professionally designed to attract the reader to the text, demonstrating careful planning and thought. Not all organizations can afford this approach. Look for simple indicators too, i.e., is the advertisement boxed? Lineage advertisements in local papers may tell you that the company is small and unsophisticated in terms of recruitment. Look at how accurately the job is described - beware of those sounding too good to be true, few jobs live up to this.

The above are key things to look out for when reading a job advertisement. Remember, read the advertisement carefully; concentrate on each aspect building up a picture as you go. If you are in any doubt, contact the company advertising the job and request further information.

Having got past the initial stages, either by filling in an application form or sending in a CV, it is now time for stage two of the process, that is presenting yourself in the best light to a prospective employer.

The employer will be looking for the person who they think best fits the role on offer. They will be looking at what you have written on your application, looking at you, how personable you are. Remember, there is, no matter what is said to the contrary, a subjective element in the interview process. Not only should you fit the paper criteria for the job but you absolutely must demonstrate personal capabilities and come across as a suitable candidate. Generally speaking, employers are interested in three main areas:

- Qualifications and skills
- Experience and background
- Personality and overall character.

These qualities can be ascertained whether the interview is a traditional face-to-face or remote. Keeping the above in mind, you should avoid the following common mistakes:

- Not answering the interview questions correctly, mumbling, not being clear or going on and on, in short waffling because you are not clear. Keep answers crisp and to the point.
- Coming across as unenthusiastic. This always turns people away very quickly. In short, your personal presentation.
- Not showing that you have studied the job description, the role on offer and the person specification. This is of the utmost importance. You must study the role before going to the interview.
- Not asking questions. At the end of the interview you will be given the chance to answer questions. Always ask pertinent questions.

- Not taking care of appearance. Be smart, whatever your personal views, as this shows initiative and self-pride.

Although it often seems that employers are looking for some kind of super person, and quite often they are, the qualities looked for by an employer will include being caring and having a helpful attitude, both to customers and colleagues. They will be looking for people who are willing and able to be part of a team, willing to take responsibility and be willing to learn. A prospective employer is about to make an investment in you and they will be expecting a return. Not unnaturally, they will be looking closely at their investment.

There is also one other point to remember. When interviewers are going about their job, it is quite often the case that they are also nervous and are unsure about the process. I know this from personal experience. They have never met you and don't know your character therefore they are feeling their way. In addition, it is not uncommon for the interviewer to feel tired and a little unenthusiastic, particularly if you are the tenth person that they have interviewed that day. Therefore, it is all the more important that you are in control of what you say, how you present yourself and the knowledge of the particular job. In this way you will impress.

Now read the main points from Chapter 1 overleaf

****

## Main Points from Chapter 1

### Employers Requirements

- Understanding the job advertisement is the key to putting together an application form or CV.

- The salary attached to a job can be misleading. Make sure that you have a clear idea of what is being offered.

- Look carefully at the company description and philosophy.

- Remember, the employer will be looking for the person who they think best fits the role on offer.

- These qualities can be ascertained whatever the form of interview.

- A prospective employer is about to make an investment and will expect a return. At this very early stage, you must get it right.

# THE INTERVIEW PROCESS-GENERAL POINTS

# Chapter 2

# The Interview Process-General Points

---

## The interview-defining an interview

An interview is a formal discussion which will enable the people interviewing to assess your skills and capabilities.

As the single biggest expense for any employer is that of recruiting and retaining staff, not unnaturally the employer will want to know that they are getting the best candidate possible for the post. Interviewing and assessing the candidate is therefore a very important part of the initial process.

## The type of interview

Not all interviews will be job interviews. Although this book is mainly concerned with job interviews, there are many types of interviews, job, college, university, voluntary work etc. What all interview situations have in common and what will be stressed throughout this book is the importance of communicating clearly, of putting yourself across in the best light and demonstrating your strengths and skills. It is the ability to present yourself, not to let yourself down which is the most important factor of interviews. This of course is underpinned by your knowledge of the field that you are trying to enter.

Until the advent of COVID 19, when you were invited to a job interview this would normally take place in front of complete strangers and would be in a private space. Interviews would come in all shapes and sizes from the informal to the formal, from a one-to-one set-up to a formal situation in front of a panel. Whatever the form of the interview the ability to impress is of utmost importance as is the ability to keep calm and be clear. After COVID it was more than likely that your interview would be over the phone, or by zoom. However, it is the case that interview situations have reverted to the more traditional type, i.e. in front of a panel. In chapter 8, we deal with interviews by phone, skype, zoom and video, which still take place, but from hereon we will discuss the more traditional form of interview.

## What takes place in an interview?

In the more traditional form of interview, when you apply for a job, if you have been short listed for an interview you will receive a letter stating what time and day the interview is on, what you should bring and what the interview will involve. The bigger the company is the more streamlined the process will be. You will usually be one of a group of people who have been selected for interview so you will almost certainly be in competition.

At the allotted time, you will be called in for interview. First impressions count. Always look smart as this shows personal initiative. Always be alert and polite and confident. These may

22

seem obvious points but they are of the utmost importance. In most cases, you will be seated at a table with the interviewers in front of you. Usually, unless the company is small, there will be more than one interviewer. You will answer questions for up to an hour, based on the job available. You will usually start off by telling the prospective employer about yourself then answer questions and ask any of your own at the end of the process.

*It is vitally important that you have a copy of your application form/CV with you so you can refer to any elements within it that an interviewer may raise.*

With all interviews, it is important to be confident and to ensure that, as it is you that will be on display and will be doing the most talking, you are in control.

Interview skills are like the skills that a person must acquire before representing themselves in court: you must prepare and be in command of the situation. However, like presenting a case in court, confidence is crucial to putting yourself across. This book will help to build up confidence as you move through the interview process.

## More complicated methods of assessment

In certain circumstances, you might have to undergo a series of tests as part of the job interview.

It is necessary, at this point, to discuss the range of tests that an employer may want you to carry out before or during the interview stage. The most common are known as psychological or psychometric tests. Not all interviews are preceded by a test of this sort, but they are becoming common enough to warrant a discussion in order to give an idea of what may be faced.

## Psychometric tests

A psychometric test is simply a standard way of measuring some specific attribute or aspect of mental behavior. It is standard because everyone who does a particular test is treated in the same way, as are the results. The idea is to produce an objective summary of what a person is or is not good at and how they come across as an individual. There are literally thousands of different tests on the market, measuring a whole different range of attributes.

Most measure one or other of the following:

- Attainment. Your learnt ability, for example what you know about arithmetic or spelling.
- Aptitude. Your ability to acquire further knowledge or skills, for example your understanding of words or ideas.
- Personality. What you are like as a person, for example, are you outgoing or quiet and thoughtful?
- Values. What you think is important, for example money or power, or both.
- Interests. What would you like to do or what activities do you think would suit you best? For example, would you prefer to fell trees or write newspaper articles.

- Skills. What you have learnt to do practically, for example there are standard tests for differing occupations.

Psychometric tests require you to answer all the questions and there is only one correct answer. You are not expected to finish in the time allowed, thereby distinguishing tests from exams. Tests can measure lots of separate abilities of which the most common are:

- Verbal ability
- Numerical ability
- Perceptual ability (understanding and reasoning)
- Spatial ability. How well you picture shapes being moved in three dimensions
- Mechanical ability
- Abstract ability. How well you can analyze a problem.
- Clerical ability. How well you understand simple arithmetic and use of English.

All these tests can be used by themselves or in combination. There are also tests for people with different levels of ability, such as those specially designed for graduates or managers.

**Personality tests**

The ancient Greeks arrived at four basic personality tests and in the twentieth century, scientists have arrived at five:

- Extrovert-introvert
- Confident-anxious
- Structured-non structured
- Conformist-non-conformist

Personality tests attempt to measure where you come on these five scales.

**Preparing for tests**

Although your early life will prepare you for tests, there are certain things that you can do to improve your performance. You should ensure that:

- You have some information about your potential employer and the sort of thing that you will be doing.
- Have an understanding what testing is like, what the experience is like.

There are many books on the market ranging from personality to I.Q tests. It is worth investing in such a book or visiting your local library (soon to be open) and spend some time doing a few selected tests. To ensure that everyone has an equal chance to do their best, most tests are administered under carefully controlled conditions. This means that you complete the tests sitting at a desk facing a test administrator (obviously this pattern will change if you are being interviewed remotely-the below refers to the traditional form of interviewing). As many tests are given to groups, you will find yourself sitting in a row, schoolroom fashion, with other candidates.

The test administrator will:

- Welcome you and introduce his/herself.
- Explain the purpose of the test.
- Detail the nature of the tests.
- Explain how the tests are to be administered.

Although most personality tests are un-timed, you are expected to finish in a reasonable time, about 35-45 minutes.

The test administrator will:

- Read out instructions for the test.
- Ask you to complete some practice questions and/or explain some worked examples.
- Tell you how much time you have for the test.
- Stop the test when appropriate and introduce the next one.
- Close the session and give you some information on what will happen next.

**Assessment of tests**

With ability tests, the employer will look to see how many questions have been answered correctly. This gives you what is known as the raw score. Your raw score is then standardized using something called a normative group. This is a large representative sample of people who have done the test in the past, including current jobholders, graduates, managers and the general population, among others.

When scores have been standardized, they can be compared on an objective basis with other people, and employers can see if you have scored above or below average and also how much above or below.

Personality tests operate in a slightly different way because there are no right or wrong answers. However, comparisons can be made within a normative group and allow employers to see, for example, if you are more or less extroverted than the average person.

Once standardized, test results can be used in one of two ways: as a source of information, which can be used at interviews or as a screening device. When results are used to screen a candidate, two further selection techniques can be used: top down or minimum cut off.

Top down means that candidates are picked on the basis of highest scores leading down. Minimum cut off selects everyone who scores over a set level.

Again, personality tests are different since it makes no sense to use top down or minimum cut off. However, candidates may be selected out if they score at the wrong extreme on a critical dimension.

If you have been tested and have been unsuccessful at this stage then the employer will always usually be prepared to give you feedback on your tests. This can often be very useful.

Now read the main points from chapter 2 overleaf.

****

## Main points from Chapter 2

The Interview Process-General Points

- The recruitment process and subsequent staff costs are the single biggest expense for an employer. Interviewing and assessing the prospective employee is therefore a crucial part of the whole process.

- Not all interviews will be job interviews, they could be for college, university etc, although this book is mainly concerned with job interviews. The principles however are the same.

- Interviews will usually be in front of total strangers and the ability to present your self well is of critical importance.

- Some jobs, particularly management jobs will have more complicated methods of assessment, such as personality tests. You will be informed of this before the interview.

- Interviews will usually be in front of several people. However, whether one or several it is very important to be smart, clear and confident and ensure that you have shown your absolute best side.

# PREPARING FOR A JOB INTERVIEW-RESEARCH AND DEVELOPMENT PRIOR TO INTERVIEW

# Chapter 3

# Planning and Preparation for a Job Interview-
# Research and Development

---

It is true to say that planning and preparation for an interview, whether face-to-face or remotely, is the most important aspect of the whole process. This initial planning informs the next stage of the process, if you are selected, which is the actual interview.

It should be obvious that if you don't make an effort researching and planning then if you get an interview, you will come across badly. You will sew the seeds of doubt in the interviewer's mind(s) and this will greatly reduce the chances of you landing the job.

Right at the outset, you should look at your work history and recap on your relevant experience and how it fits in with the role that you are applying for. You need to look at any discrepancies in your work history and put these in a positive light. For example, you may have taken time out to go travelling. Make sure that you explain this clearly and weave it in as part of your overall experience.

**Researching the employer**

It is vitally important that you carry out at least some research on the potential employer. If the organisation has a website make sure that you access it to glean as much information as possible about the company. Make sure that you have at least an idea of the following:

- What does the employer do - i.e., what do they make, what do they supply, what is their reason for being?
- Importantly, what is the mission statement of the company. If you have knowledge about this at an interview it will stand you in good stead.
- If the organisation is a public sector employer how well are they regarded and what can be your contribution to their overall performance?
- What kind of skills do you think they are seeking?

Make sure that you are thoroughly conversant with the company and their operations and make sure that you convey this knowledge if you get to the interview stage.

**Researching the organisation**

As we have highlighted, the first stage of planning is to gather as much information as you can about the prospective employer. Pay very careful attention to the job description that you have been sent along with the person specification if you have one. Don't ignore this as employers will expect the application form to be filled in, in accordance with the person specification. In addition, it is highly likely that an interview will be designed around the person specification.

You're thinking and acting will be very much informed by your initial research. If you find that you don't exactly fit the person specification then ensure that you can provide enough information about your background and experience to compensate for this.

We discussed the fact that a large part of an interview is subjective. This is because we are human beings and an employer will need to know that you can fit in with all concerned, in addition to fulfilling your role. Being able to fit the person specification absolutely perfectly is not the be-all and end-all. The interviewer will also, whether consciously or unconsciously, be looking at you as a person.

It is up to you to sell yourself at an interview. You are all you have and it is important to be confident and to come across well.

## Analysing the role on offer-the Job description

When you first receive the employment pack (usually there will be a pack unless the employer is small) there are crucial first steps that you should take:

- Work carefully through the job description-make sure that you understand it.
- Highlight the main activities of the role.
- As you go through make notes about the experience you have and how it relates to the role on offer.
- Keep clear notes, typing them up at the end of the process.

**Person Specification**

You will find out that larger companies, public sector organisations and the Civil Service will include a person specification. This will be divided into essential and non-essential requirements, based around experience and qualifications. For example, if you intend to work in housing management then the essential requirements might be a qualification in housing management. The experience might be at least two years as a housing manager in a large organisation or similar. Non-essential requirements might be a working knowledge of IT packages. A willingness to learn is just as important.

When studying the person specification, make sure:

- That you work through each of the areas carefully making notes about the relevance of these to your experience. Relate them to your own background.
- Make sure that you then complete the application form with the person specification as guidance. This is crucial and if you don't you won't get to the interview stage. You will be wasting your time.

**The interview**

Give a lot of thought, after you have filled in the application form, about the actual job. Think about the qualities required, the skills and experience and the main areas of questioning that are likely to arise in an interview. There are three main areas of questioning:

- Your qualifications and skills
- Your previous work experience
- Your character and personality.

## Qualifications and skills

When filling in your application form, you will have stated your qualifications. It is important at the interview to have a copy of the application form. Don't try to do it by memory. What you say will have to accord exactly with the application form. If you haven't taken any qualifications then you should ensure that you are in a position to elaborate on your school and/or your college background.

## Previous work experience

Your work experience, and your demonstration of this is obviously very important. This should be prominent on the application form and also at the front of your mind. Although your jobs will be highlighted it is important that you can elaborate on these and ensure that what you are saying helps to give the interviewer a clearer picture of your experience. What IT packages did you use, or can you use? What contact did you have with the public and what are your customer service skills.

In short, what are the skills that are transferable to the role for which you are applying?

## You as an individual

As we discussed, the employer will attach great importance to the type of person that you are, how you conduct yourself, your attitude towards others and your approach to teamwork. It is not enough in an interview to trot out the same old answers when asked about yourself. It is important to actually demonstrate your character. An awful lot is happening on a subconscious and conscious level at an interview and it is crucial to present your self in the best light.

Always be positive about your previous employment. Never come across as cynical or jaded about a previous employer. Never show bitterness if, for example, you have been made redundant from a post or have had problems with managers. It is all history and an employer is looking at how you will get on in the future in their organisation.

## End of interview

At the end of the interview, you will always be asked if you have any questions. You should always ask questions as this shows initiative and keenness. If you can't think of any then you should state clearly that you think that all the important points have been covered but if you have any questions later then you will contact them. There are certain questions that you shouldn't ask relating to pay and conditions as these will have been set out in

38

the original documentation that is sent. If this hasn't been pointed out or salary is subject to negotiation leave this until the job has been offered. The questions should relate specifically to the company or to the role. See Chapter 6 for more about interview questions.

Now read the main points from Chapter 3 overleaf.

**\*\*\*\***

# Main points from Chapter 3

## Planning and Preparation

- Planning and preparation for an interview is the most important aspect of the whole process.
- You should recap on all your relevant experience and how it fits in with the role that you are applying for.
- It is vitally important that you carry out at least some research into the potential employer.
- Pay very careful attention to the job description and person specification if you have been sent one.
- Always have a copy of the application form/CV with you at the interview.

# PRESENTING MATERIAL IN AN INTERVIEW- INTERVIEW- PRESENTATION SKILLS

# Chapter 4

# Making a Presentation in an Interview-a Few Tips

---

**Types of presentation**

The types of presentation that you may be asked to carry out in a job interview include:

- Prepare and present a five-minute outline of your ideas for developing the job role.
- Prepare a 15-minute presentation on one of the likely priorities in the job.
- Give a talk for ten minutes on the main issues likely to affect this organisation.
- Explain in 15 minutes the SWOT (strengths weaknesses opportunities and threats) facing the organisation.

Whatever type of presentation you are asked to do, particularly if it is a verbal and visual presentation, you will need to bear a few main points in mind. These are outlined below.

**Personal skills-Body Language**

People have a natural ability to use body language together with speech. Body language emphasizes speech and enables us to communicate more effectively with others. It is vitally important when preparing for a presentation to understand the nature of your body language and also to connect this to another all-important element-*vision*.

## Vision

People tend to take in a lot of information with their eyes and obviously presentations are greatly enhanced by use of visual aids. Together, when presenting to a group of people, *body language and visual stimuli* are all important. A great amount of thought needs to go into the elements of what it is that you are about to present and the way you intend to convey your message. What you should not do, especially as a novice, is to stand up in front of a group and deliver a presentation off the top of your head. You need to carry out thorough research into what it is you are presenting and to whom you are presenting.

## Developing a style

Every person will have his or her own style. At one end of the spectrum there are those people who give no thought to what it is they are doing and have no real interest in the audience. For them it is a chore and one which should be gotten over as soon as is possible. Here, there is a definite absence of style.

At the other end of the spectrum are those who have given a great deal of thought to what they are doing, given a great deal of thought to their material and have a genuine interest in the audience. Such speakers will be greatly stimulating and leave a lasting impression and convey something of some worth.

Underlying all of this is your *own personal style*, partly which develops from an understanding of the above and partly from an understanding of yourself. Some presenters of material recognize their own speed of presentation, i.e., slow, medium, or fast and also understand their own body language. Some are more fluent than others, use their hands more etc. Having recognized your own style what you need to do is to adjust your own way of presentation to the specific requirements of the occasion. The key point is to gain attention, get the message across and be stimulating to a degree.

All of the above considerations begin to translate themselves into a style that you yourself will begin to recognize and feel comfortable with. Once this occurs you will find that, when presenting, your nerves will begin to melt away and your confidence begins to develop.

## Formal presentations

There is not one particular style appropriate to public speaking. Each occasion will merit its own approach. However, there are a few commonly observed rules.

## Use of language

The use of language is a specific medium that must be understood when making a presentation. Obviously, if you are speaking publicly to a group of familiar people who know and understand you, a different approach will be needed and a different form of language, perhaps less formal, utilized than that used in front of a group who are totally unfamiliar.

Nevertheless, using formal but simple language interspersed with funny remarks is undoubtedly one of the best ways to approach any form of audience. You should certainly avoid too much detail and do not go overboard with funny comments as this will become tedious. Stick to the subject matter lightening up the occasion with a few anecdotes and witty comments. It is all about the right blend and pitch.

**More about body language**

We have briefly discussed body language. It is astounding how much you can tell about people in the street by simply observing their body language. Usually, people form an impression about another within the first five minutes of meeting. It is essential, in a public speaking situation that your body language should reflect a confident personality with a good sense of humour. In order to achieve this, you should think about the following:

- Use of hands- Use your hands to emphasize what you say and to invite the audience to accept your point
- Keep your hands open and keep your fingers open.
- Avoid putting your hands in your pocket and avoid losing them. Firmly avoid pointing fingers
- Co-ordinate your hand movements with your words.

## Using facial expressions

People tend to concentrate on the face of a public speaker, in addition to the movements of the body. Obviously, your face, along with body language is a vehicle for expression. A smile every now and again is important. There are other actions that can help:

- Use of eyebrows for inviting people to accept your ideas.
- Moving the head to look at all members of a group. It is very important indeed to maintain a sense of involvement on the part of all.
- Do not fix your eyes on one place or person for long. This will isolate the rest of the audience and may be interpreted as nervousness or a lack of confidence on your part.
- Look at individuals every time you mention something in their area of expertise or are singling them out in a positive way.
- Look at people even if they appear not to be looking at you.

*The face is a very important part of the communication apparatus and the use of this part of the body is of the utmost importance when public speaking.*

## Controlling your movements

In addition to the use of face and hands the way you move can have an effect on your audience. Your movements can vary from standing rigid and fixed to acting out roles and being fluid generally. There are, in keeping with body language generally, certain rules relating to movement:

Restrict your movements only to those that are most necessary. Avoid throwing yourself all over the place and distracting people's attention from the emphasis of your presentation

Always face the people that you are addressing. Never look at the floor or away from the audience, at least not for a prolonged period.

## Dress

When adopting the role of public speaker, it is very important to be dressed formally and in accordance with the standard of the occasion. People must be impressed. This means that you must give thought to what you wear, how you can help to achieve a sense of control through dress.

## Attitude

Your attitude is crucial to your success in public speaking. Attitudes can be greatly influenced by nerves and by being ill - prepared. There is nothing worse than a public speaker who slowly degenerates into aggression or hostility through sarcasm or other forms of attack. Yet this is all too frequent.

At all times you must maintain a professional and formal attitude that allows you to remain in control. You can think yourself into this state if you find yourself slipping or feel that you are losing control. If you feel that you are straying in any way then you should get back on course. This can be achieved through a number of ways such as by changing the subject slightly in order to give yourself time to gather your wits or by asking the group to refocus on the subject in question.

## Formalities

Another fundamental rule of presentations is the way you open or introduce the presentation and the way you close. When public speaking, it is always necessary to introduce yourself even if most of the audience know who you are. It is vital that everyone knows who you are and what you are there for. Having got these necessary formalities over with, the audience will feel more comfortable listening to you because they now have a point of reference.

## Effective delivery

Good delivery of a speech is a matter of being confident that you can remember what to say, and when and how you want to say it. It is also about communicating with an audience, not only through what you say, but through the attitude of your body, and by the expression of your voice. Good delivery, like a good speaking style, can be learned through adequate rehearsal and control of your nerves.

## First impressions

 As discussed earlier, when you first move into a person's field of vision, they make an instant judgment on your appearance. The same thing happens when you first move in front of an audience. The style of your dress will mark you out, whether you are smartly dressed or whether you are casual or wearing a particular mode of dress that puts you into a particular slot, dress has a 'tribal' effect and people will categorize you on the spot.

Take advantage of these common perceptions in order to put the audience in the right frame of mind to listen to your speech. Be smartly dressed and avoid wearing anything that is outlandish. Pay attention to detail. Do not overdress. This can also distract your audience from your material.

### Eye contact

It would be useful to watch an actor when they are making eye contact and to try to work out what it is they are doing with their eyes. In most cases, the actor is doing his or her level best to avoid looking into the eyes of another person.

By making eye contact, we are expressing our openness towards other people. We are also showing that we are not frightened of them and that we are interested in their feelings, thoughts and reactions. When the contact is made, a direct line of communication is opened up and the listener's attention is held. Making eye contact with an audience is one of the most valuable skills that a speaker can learn. Eye contact can be practiced in almost any social situation, and you will be surprised how it changes people's reaction to you. They will become more attentive and more willing to trust what it is you have to say.

They will begin to look upon you as a more approachable person-exactly the kind of response that you want from your audience.

When you are speaking to a group, avoid picking out one single member of the audience and making eye contact exclusively with him or her. This will make that person very uncomfortable and the rest of the audience will begin to feel excluded. Make eye contact with different individuals round the room so that you take in the whole audience.

If you are inexperienced and nervous, you may not wish to make eye contact straight away. In this case, deliver your first couple of lines to a point above the audience's head. However, as soon as the time is appropriate, start making eye contact. This should come as you feel more confident.

You will find that if you have opted to read your speech from a script, it will be very difficult to make time to make eye contact. Eye contact is central to delivering your message in a personal and effective way and, for this reason, it is important to free your eyes from the written word.

## Presenting visual aids

If you have incorporated any form of visual aid into your presentation, you will need to pay particular attention to your body language. Your first consideration should be to not allow the visual aid to come between you and your audience. Too many speakers bend down and read overhead transparencies or turn their backs on the audience to see which slide comes next.

However great the temptation to do otherwise, always speak to the audience, and not to the equipment. You will help yourself if you make it a rule never to operate the visual equipment whilst speaking.

The second problem with presenting visual aids is that they present untold opportunities for nervous speakers to fiddle. If you have to change a transparency or reveal an exhibit, do so with as little extra movement as possible. Make sure that before you start speaking, your transparencies are in order and if you need something to point with it is to hand.

**Practicing presentations**

*Consider all of the above and then practicing.* This is the absolute key to successful presentations and to effective public speaking. Practice most certainly lifts your confidence level up and assists you in staying in control The more time and effort that you spend practicing the less that you will have to worry about when presenting. Let's face it, a presentation is a live stage show. How do stand up comic's feel when they expose themselves to an audience? Develop a practicing technique by trying different methods:

- You should choose a topic that you are very interested in and prepare a short presentation on it.
- Stand in front of a mirror and present to yourself. Repeat this over and over observing different aspects of your style.

- Try to rectify any bad habits.
- Experiment with various styles and techniques until you find one that suits you.
- Try to film yourself if possible. Replay the film and observe yourself. This is one of the most effective ways of changing your style or developing your style.
- Ask a friend to observe you and to make detailed criticism. Do not be afraid of criticism as this is always constructive.

Finally, It may be that you will be asked to carry out exercises which will not entail you actually doing a presentation. You may, for example, have to carry out an in-tray exercise, or other exercises which will test your ability to prioritise. You may also be involved in discussions, particularly where a high level of people contact or management is central to the job.

Bearing in mind that we are in a situation where more often than not the interviews will be remote, at least in the short term, then the main points presented in this chapter should be adapted, where possible, to your situation.

Now read the key points from Chapter 4 overleaf.

****

# Main Points from Chapter 4

## Presentations

- The types of presentation that you may be asked to carry out will vary from short to lengthy and will usually relate directly to the organisation and the job.

- There are a number of key areas which should be remembered when presenting-body language, vision, style, use of language, facial expressions, dress and attitude.

- Always make eye contact generally when presenting, avoid singling people out.

- Try to practice presentations before you go for your interview.

# THE DAY OF THE INTERVIEW

# Chapter 5

# The Day of the Interview
# Some Main Points.

---

**The interview**

You do not get to the interview stage unless the employer believes that you can do the job. This means that you have already been accepted on the basis of your C.V or application. You supply all the information about yourself. This means that while the interviewer controls the structure of the interview, decisions can only be made on the basis of what you provide.

Most of the interview questions can be predicted in advance. This being the case, you can prepare answers in your own time, answers which cast you in the most positive light. Before we look at interview tactics, it is useful to know that there are a number of different types of face-to-face interview. For the moment we will exclude remote Interviews.

There are three main variations:

- Single. This is a one to one meeting between the interviewer and candidate. Of all the types of interviews, it is the most relaxing for both interviewer and interviewee alike. This type of interview is favored by smaller organizations although there can be a potential for bias.

- Sequential interview. This is where there is a series of interviews, usually two or maybe three, carried out by different interviewers. It allows for a range of impressions to be gathered.

Although in theory this process should be more democratic, in practice the most senior interviewer will have the most sway.

- Panel interview. This involves being questioned by a number of interviewers, in turn, at the same interview. This type of interview is popular in most organizations and the number of interviewers varies. The type of person(s) interviewing will vary depending on the type of organization.

**The facts about interviews**

The latest figures show that 90% of organizations use interviews. Interviewers will make up their mind quite rapidly, usually after the first four or five minutes. Making a positive first impression is very important indeed. Different interviewers set different standards. They pay attention to information that is out of the ordinary and are more influenced by negative information than positive. Interviewers are not very good at assessing real personality. This is not really possible in such a short space of time. Characteristics often begin to manifest themselves several weeks into the job. How you are judged during and after an interview depends very much on who the interviewer has seen. This is known technically as the Halo effect.

There are many other points about interviews which we have already mentioned, a main one being that subjectivity will creep in, i.e., how well your face fits, whether you are considered to be a team player and so on. At the end of the day, you have to fit into the organization and those interviewing will only employ you if this is perceived to be the case.

## Preparing for interviews

Although some of the negative aspects of the interview process have been stressed, you should always try to be positive. You need to pay a lot of attention to preparing for the interview, whether the interview is face-to-face or whether it is remote. A few preliminary points need to be considered:

- Do you know exactly where and what time the interview is taking place? This may sound silly, but in your initial excitement and haste, you may overlook it until the last moment and may find yourself at a disadvantage.
- Do you know who is going to be interviewing you, their name and job title?

Do you know enough about the organization, have you researched them, and do you know enough about their history and product?

## Personal presentation

As was discussed in the last chapter, this is of the utmost importance. What you wear will have to be appropriate to the type of business you are dealing with. You are going to a business meeting so you should wear the smartest clothes that you can and dress conservatively. Dark colors have a greater impact.

The main point here is that you should not disadvantage yourself, no matter what your outlook on life. You may secretly hate wearing a suit and tie but in order to get the job you want you have to bend to the whims of the employer. This is just as important in these days of the remote interview, not so much the telephone interview but the Zoom or video interview.

Remember, they have the power in this situation, and you have to prove yourself.

## Materials

Don't forget to take your C.V or application to the interview. Also take a pen and paper for taking notes. Try to prepare some questions to ask the interviewers when the interview is over.

## Making an Impression

As mentioned, research has shown that interviewers usually make up their minds during the first few minutes and spend the rest of the interview trying to confirm this impression. First impressions are based on several things: what you look like and how you behave. The impression that you make will, to a large degree, depend on the interviewer and his or her prejudices and dislikes and overall bias.

## Body language

We talked at length about preparation, including body language. This bit will require some practice. Obviously, your body language will vary depending on the situation you are in, those in front of you and how you feel at the time. The impression that you will make will rest on:

- Facial expression and how you move your head.
- What you do with your hands and arms.
- What you do with the rest of your body.

It is also useful to know that, in terms of being believable, the most accurate signals someone gives out are such things as going pale, swallowing and sweating, which are automatic, followed by what you do with your legs and feet and the rest of your body. A few important points:

- Look at the interviewer and smile.
- Keep your hands away from your face.
- Nod your head to show that you are paying attention.
- Lean forward when speaking and back when listening.

*At the same time:*

- Do not make sudden movements.
- Do not fold your arms.

In particular, sit in a relaxed manner and do not fidget. This means do not move about on the seat and keep your feet and hands still. You need to give the interviewer the impression of being business-like and confident, genuinely interested in the position on offer.

### The structure of the interview

At the outset, the interviewer will try to relax you and break the ice. An effort will be made to explain the interview process to you. There is a fairly common format to the interview process, and they will normally tie into the C.V or application form. The interviewer will begin by talking about the organization and its history and future plans. Then you will be invited to tell the interviewer(s) about your own recent work history and how it fits in with the job on offer. They may even ask you at this stage why you have applied for the post although this normally comes later.

Generally, the questions related to the post will begin at this time. The interviewers will ask you structured questions. Usually, candidates for a job will get asked the same questions. This, however, will vary depending on the post, the organization and other factors. The next chapter outlines a range of questions that you might be asked.

Now read the main points from Chapter 5 overleaf.

****

## Main points from Chapter 5

### The Day of the Interview

- You will not get to the interview stage unless the employer believes that you can fill the post.

- There are three main types of interviews-or variations on the theme: Single or one-to-one interviews; sequential interviews and panel interviews.

- Interviews are usually highly subjective so you must always show yourself in the best light.

- This is relevant to face-to-face interviews and remote interviews, particularly zoom or video interviews.

# Chapter 6

# Answering Interview Questions

___

Without doubt, the longest part of a job interview will be the time taken to answer questions put to the candidate. This is also the most stressful part of the interview process. The main worry is whether you can answer questions clearly, indeed do you know the answers? Are you as good as the next candidate and so on. The key to answering the questions is to have as much knowledge in advance of the questions and to have comprehensively prepared the answers.

It is, of course, impossible to predict questions in the interview setting. However, having considered the nature of the post then a guesstimate of the questions can be made.

You should think about the question from the employer's point of view. Employers will get straight to the point and will ask questions relevant to the job. The questions will rarely be trick questions, unless the person interviewing doesn't have a clear idea of what they should be asking or hasn't done the required preparation. If a job description or person specification has been sent then it is almost certain that these will form the basis for the questioning.

The interviewer(s) will usually always start with a question to the candidate asking them to elaborate on their background. This will give the interviewers a chance to get a feel of the person and whether or not they have the necessary experience and educational qualifications.

Although this has been written on your application form now is the chance to elaborate. In addition, questions are likely to be asked about hobbies and outside interests. Other, more general questions will explore attitudes and abilities plus maybe questions on the way the candidate might approach the role if the job was offered.

Although each job is different and therefore the range of questions will be different, there are particular formats that interviews tend to follow and a range of questions that, in one form or another, might appear. Listed below are certain questions that you may encounter. I have categorised the areas into education and training, employment, personal interests and so on. You will rarely be asked all the questions but it is better to be prepared and have as wide range of answers as possible.

**Education and training**

*Question-When you left school you decided to take a course of further education at college. Can you tell us why you did this?*

You will need to think about your way of thinking at the time, why you decided to go to college and what qualifications you hoped to get.

The main thing to show here is that you didn't go to college because you had no other options or that you didn't merely drift into college but that you had clear ideas of what you were doing at the time.

*Question-Can you tell us more about the course that you did at college?*

It is important that you are clear here and can give concise answers. Employers are looking for initiative. Were there aspects of the course that you completed which might be relevant to the post on offer?

Although you might have included this information on your CV or application form the employer may not have it to hand and will want you to elaborate. Given that the course at college may have ended a long time ago then you should ensure that you have this information to hand.

*Question-Can you tell us about a particular project that you worked on at school?*

Because the world of work revolves around projects of one sort of another, from management to administration, this question is designed to see if you are task orientated, how practical you are and whether you have had any early experiences of team or group work which would be relevant to the job.

**Employment history**

This area of questioning will relate directly to your work history and will concentrate on jobs that you have already held.

***Question-Have you had work experience?*** As can be gathered, this type of question is usually asked younger candidates, those who have had very little experience of a job, outside of Saturday jobs. It is not enough to say that you are completely inexperienced and have only just left school. You will need to explore your part time roles, when you were at school, such as a paper round, Saturday work in a chain store and so on.

The idea is to convey the fact that you have varied experience and so can slot into the world of work. If you have never held down any type of job before then now is the time to start as employers are most definitely unimpressed by those who have never bothered to get some kind of work. You can undertake voluntary work in the community, work in a charity shop indeed do any one of a number of jobs that will at least give you experience.

***Question-Can you tell us more about your last job?*** You will need to summarise the main areas of your last job so that the interviewers get a clear idea of what you were doing and how it relates to the post on offer.

You will need to give some advance thought to this and ensure that you bring out the areas most relevant to the post.

Explain how you carried out the main tasks and give examples where appropriate to illustrate the tasks and the role.

**Question-Why did you leave your last job?** This is an area that needs careful answering. There are many reasons why you might have left the job. You might have been sacked. You might have resigned due to disagreements with managers or for a whole host of other reasons.

You might just have reached the end of that particular job cycle, felt that there were no further challenges and need to move on. Whatever the reason, you must come across as positive and not give the interviewers the idea that you are difficult and can't get along with people or that you are not likely to stay long in the post. If you are currently employed ensure that you convey the fact that you are leaving or want to leave to better yourself.

**Question-What have you been doing since you left your last job?** If there has been a period between jobs, the employer will want to know how this has been used. This is an area that can be turned to your advantage. If you have been unemployed for a while, you must be able to explain clearly what it is you have been doing, apart from looking for another job.

The best answer will be that you have been undertaking a course of study to improve your skills or that you have been doing voluntary work. It might also be possible to state that you have been doing some freelance work. The most important thing to show is initiative and that you were not merely idling the time away.

**Question-*Can you tell us briefly what has been one of your significant achievements in your last job?***
This is the kind of question that will require some thought. Always give some time to this. The example that you give should contain some of the main qualities, or demonstrate those qualities, that are needed in your current job.

**Question-*Can you tell us briefly about problems that you have had to deal with?*** This type of question is asked in order to get you to demonstrate what your attitude to obstacles is. Again, this type of question requires thought on your part and you should draw out an example that portrays you as a successful problem solver. The problem could be people based or resource based. Whatever it is, ensure that you present yourself as positive and a solution orientated person.

**Question-*What would you do if faced with a difficult customer posing problems that you couldn't deal with?*** This type of question is asked to enable interviewers to assess your ability to handle customers and to provide them with the best care that you can. It is very important that you get this right. In a case like this you would deal with the person calmly, listen carefully, never respond like for like, never run your organisation down, offer apologies and tell the customer that you will discuss the matter with a supervisor. Remember, the question is what you would do if you can't deal with the problem. In this case, after placating the customer you would refer the matter to your supervisor.

**Question-*Which of your jobs have you found the most interesting and why?*** This question might be asked if you have had a varied employment history with different jobs. It is designed to assess what you like the most and what you actively dislike.

Again, give some thought to this question and ensure that you answer it in the light of the job on offer.

**Question-*What hobbies and personal interests do you have?*** This kind of question is designed to gain an impression of the type of person you are and what you enjoy doing in your spare time. As with all the other questions, you should give some thought to this. If you have unusual hobbies, such as riding your Harley Davidson down to Brighton on a bank holiday weekend, make sure that you come across as a team orientated person with a love of motorcycles. This demonstrates that you are a person with initiative and that you enjoy the company of people.

You do not need to be too specific about religious or political interests or bother mentioning those pastimes that most of us enjoy, such as watching television, going out with friends etc. It is the more specific hobbies that matter. Make sure that you include a variety of interests, some of these involving the use of the mind, others more physical. Try to include at least one pastime that is unusual and will invite more questions. Be prepared to discuss these in detail.

**General questions**

**Question-*What do you feel are your main strengths?***

Make sure that you give thought to this and make sure that you shine. This is the type of question that will either put you in a very good light or put you in a bad light. You should think carefully and list your main strengths. It might seem an easy thing to do but it is harder than you think.

Examples of strengths can be that you are punctual, keep to deadlines, flexible, work well under pressure, are diplomatic and so on. It is quite likely that the interviewer might ask you to elaborate on one or other of the strengths, for example, 'can you tell us more about the diplomatic side of yourself, give us an example of this in action'. Remember, although it might seem easy to describe your strengths, you should have a clear idea of what they are and also be prepared to give an example. One way of preparing for a question like this is to list your strengths.

Overleaf is a table in which you should compile a list of ten strengths.

Your ten strengths.

| | |
|---|---|
| 1. | |
| 2. | |
| 3. | |
| 4. | |
| 5. | |
| 6. | |
| 7. | |
| 8. | |
| 9. | |
| 10. | |

When you list the strengths make sure that they are considered and that they don't come across as mere boasts.

**Question-*What are your weaknesses?*-**This is a tricky question and should be considered carefully. If you do mention any weakness at all then make sure that it sounds like a strength. For example, "I sometimes take my work too seriously and spend long hours at the office, rather than going home and relaxing. I am aware of this and will try to ensure that I get on top of it". In this way you have shown that your only real weakness is your over-dedication to your work.

**Question-*Which current affairs problems have you been aware of recently?*** This question is designed to gauge your awareness of the wider world and your interest. It will usually arise in the context of public service jobs. It will also help the interviewer to assess your political attitudes. Employers rarely want candidates to express strong political views at interviews. This is certainly true of the Civil Service and local authorities. Generally, someone who expresses strong political views will make the interviewer seem uncomfortable as they might think that they have to engage you in debate. In addition, if you are applying for a local authority job then you will  be required to work for an authority that is led by parties from the left, right or centre.

Make sure that you read up on affairs by buying a quality newspaper and you are at least up to speed.

### Question-*What do you see yourself doing in five years time?*

This question requires thought. Why should an interviewer ask this and what are they trying to gauge? What they are generally trying to do is to assess what your ambitions are and how long you are thinking of staying in the job. You should always answer in the context of furthering your career in the organisation and that you hope to give the best of yourself in service of that organisation. Don't be vague and never give the impression that you will move on as soon as you tire of the job.

### Question-*Why should we employ you as opposed to another Candidate?* This is a question where you can bring in your strengths as listed earlier. Employers are interested in listening about your skills, experience, and your personality. You should answer this in a measured way, not coming across as boastful

74

and not running down any other candidate. However, although you should avoid being boastful you should, at the same time, sell yourself as hard as possible. This will give the impression of confidence.

You can bring your own ideas in also, your view of the organisation, its future, and your role in it and what you can give. Obviously, the question will be easier or harder to answer depending on the job on offer, whether it is a senior or junior role, a specialised role, or a more common role.

**Question-*What does equal opportunities/diversity mean to you and how would you put this into practice?*** This question is the most difficult one to answer and always taxes minds. It is all too easy to trot out a standard answer such as 'It mean equal opportunities for all' or 'It redresses imbalances in opportunity'. None of these hit the mark or get to the heart of the question.

Think carefully, why should the interviewer be asking this question and of what relevance is it? Generally speaking, equal opportunities policies exist in most organisations now. Whereas many years ago, when in its infancy, equal opportunities questions could be answered relatively simply. Nowadays, the whole concept and practice is a little more complicated.

At the heart of the answer should be your awareness that an equal opportunities policy exists to ensure that opportunities within the organisation are available to all regardless of race, colour, creed, religion, sexuality, or gender. The origins of policies lie here. However, it is now also the case that such polices cover diversity, which is ensuring that people of all cultures are respected for their diversity, for example, religious difference, cultural differences etc.

It is true to say that some people are very zealous about these policies and will be looking for answers that are very clearly articulated and demonstrate a true understanding. Therefore, you should study the organisations policy before going for interview and also ensure that you have a full grasp of the meaning.

**The actual job on offer**

**Question-*Tell us what you know about this organisation?* This** question will often arise and there is no excuse for you not knowing anything about the organisation and its operations. You should have carefully studied the facts and figures, the methods and operations and, in particular, the mission statement (if the organisation has one). Search the internet for any information that might be offered. The larger the company the more certain it is that they will have a website dedicated to the company. Make sure that you absorb all aspects of the company and its product, its performance, and its targets. Knowing about the company will also help you put the job in context and will put you in a good light when going for an interview.

***Question-Why do you want to work for this particular company?*** The answer to this question depends on the type of work being offered and how much you know about the company. You should always give the impression that you want to work for the company because you respect what they do and how they do it. Never give the impression that you are only looking for a job and don't particularly care for the company, or any other company for that matter.

**Question-*What do you think are the most important issues facing this organisation at this moment in time?*** This question will test your knowledge of the company and of the political, social and financial environment affecting the company at the time. Again, when you research the company you can get clues. Your answer will also demonstrate that you read newspapers.

In addition, your answer would depend on the nature of the organisation but can include income generation, recession, allocating scarce resources, setting clear objectives, cutbacks in staff, quality control and so on. The issues could be numerous and you should be in a position to articulate them.

At the end of the questions, you will normally be told about the terms and conditions, and also about the interview process, i.e. when they expect to be able to make a decision.

There are many variations on the above theme. During the course of the interview, the person(s) interviewing may decide to concentrate more on you and ask you about your aspirations. You should always be cautious here and appear ambitious but not unrealistic. If your employer thinks that they cannot meet your aspirations, then it may cost you your job. They may try to gauge your interests and your circumstances in order to build up a clearer picture of you and try to get a picture of your background.

This very much depends on the job and interviewers. It is the practice in the public sector, for example, to try to remain as objective as possible, also in larger private sector organizations. However, this may differ radically in other organizations depending on size, nature of the operation and so on.

There are a few golden rules in interviews. Never get too aggressive or arrogant in front of the interviewers. This can happen for a number of reasons. It can be down to nervousness, insecurity or the fact that you are doing badly, or at least you feel you are and try to mask this by being hostile or aggressive.

If you fall into this mode of behavior, then you will almost certainly not get the job. If you feel that you cannot answer a question, then you should ask the person to go back to it later. This will give you more time to focus your mind and relax.

Earlier, we talked about preparation. Part of preparation is mental preparation. Putting you into the right frame of mind and becoming confident. If you stop to think about it, all you are doing is sitting in front of people who work for a firm, who wish you no harm and want to see you succeed. If you think yourself into this frame of mind, then even if you get the idea that you are not doing well then you can still retain your self-confidence and dignity.

Now read the main points from Chapter 6 overleaf.

****

## Main points from Chapter 6

Answering Interview Questions

- The longest part of a job interview will be the time taken to answer questions put to the candidates.

- You should take time to consider what questions will be asked, in the light of the job on offer.

- Interviewers will always start with a question to the candidate asking them to elaborate on their background.

- There are particular formats that interviewers tend to follow- as have been elaborated in this chapter.

# Chapter 7

# How Do Interviewers Make Decisions?

---

A good interviewer will assess you against the requirements for the job. This means that your particular skills, abilities, experiences and knowledge will be matched against a list of essential and desirable qualities. It might be that a particular sort of business experience is required and ideally the employer is seeking certain types of qualifications. The list is known as the person specification, and the better the fit between you and the person specification the greater the chances of getting the job.

This makes it sound simple, in reality however the process is quite complicated. The reason for this is that certain sorts of information appear to be more influential than others. The following factors are seen to be particularly influential:

- Personality. How you present yourself as a person.
- Experience. The experience you have that is relevant to the job.
- Qualifications. The qualifications that you have which are relevant to the job.
- Background. Your general work background and your track record.

- Enthusiasm. How motivated and interested you appear to be about the job.
- Education. Your general level of educational experience.

This list reinforces the critical need to make a powerful and positive impression on the employer. It also stresses the need to relate experience, qualifications and general work background to the job in question and give the impression that you are an energetic and motivated individual with a genuine interest in the work and the employer's organization.

Whatever the method of assessing the information or the weight given to it, the end result is that you will eventually be offered a job or turned down. This process takes time and during this period another part of the selection system comes into operation. The employer will offer the job to the best candidate but the second or even the third will not be rejected. Someone is always kept in reserve in case the first candidate rejects the job offer.

In general, if you have not heard anything after ten days, contact the employer and ask if a decision has been made. Sometimes, people are actually offered a job at an interview. If this happens to you, remember that it could mean a number of things:

- The employer is very impressed.
- You have undersold yourself.
- The employer is desperate.

In relation to underselling yourself, you should leave all salary negotiations to the end of the selection process. If you are asked what you expect to be paid, give a range and ask what the rate for the job is. The point is that you are in a much more powerful negotiating position when someone actually wants you and genuinely believes that you are the best person for the job.

## Reading the signs

Before the final decision, you can get some indication of your performance if you consider what happened at the interview. Positive signs include:

- Any detailed discussions about salary.
- Any exploration of when you can start the job.
- An interview that lasts longer than expected.
- An interview, which includes unscheduled meetings with other decision makers, such as managers.
- Being invited to a second interview.

In contrast, negative signs are:

- An interview, which is much shorter than anticipated, perhaps only 20 minutes long.
- Being repeatedly caught out by the interviewer and not being able to answer the questions.
- An obvious clash between your personal requirements and what the company can provide, for example in terms of work hours.

After the interview, if you have been turned down, you should contact the company and try to get feedback from the interview. This can be invaluable and put you on the right track for the next interview.

Now read the main points from Chapter 7 overleaf.

****

# Main points from Chapter 7

## How do Interviewers Make Decisions?

- A good interviewer will assess you against the requirements for the job.

- There are a number of factors seen to be influential in a job interview: personality, job experience, qualifications and education, background and enthusiasm.

- There are a number of signs which can indicate whether or not you have been successful in the job interview

*Remember, it is up to you to present yourself in the best light!*

# Chapter 8

# How to Perform Well in Remote Interviews

---

## What are Remote Interviews?

They are real interviews held over the phone or by methods such as Zoom/Skype or by video, rather than face-to-face. Remote interviews have been much more common during the pandemic. You will usually be interviewed by a member of the graduate recruitment or HR team. In normal times, a telephone interview will usually be given to candidates who have passed the online application and/or psychometric test stage of the graduate recruitment process and is used to sift out applicants to be invited to a face-to-face interview or assessment centre. May of the principles applying to Skype also apply to Zoom.

## Who uses telephone interviews?

You are more likely to have a telephone interview with one of the large corporate recruiters than with a small or medium sized company. Telephone interviews are used by all kinds of employers – banks, accountancy and law firms, consultancies, retailers, manufacturing companies etc. Companies that use telephone interviews include Tesco, HSBC, Corus, BT, Lloyds of

London, Shell, GlaxoSmithKline, Vodaphone, BSkyB and many others.

They are especially common for sales-related jobs, such as recruitment consultancy and particularly (surprise!) telesales, where verbal communication skills are paramount. You may also expect a telephone interview if you are applying for jobs abroad – in which case calls may come in at all hours of the day or night!

## How long do they last?

Based on a small sample of people who have had telephone interviews, they varied in length from 20 minutes to 1 hour, with the average length being half an hour:

## Advantages of telephone interviews

For the employer:

- They are time and cost-effective - most last about 20-25 minutes.
- They test your verbal communication skills and telephone technique.

For you:

- You can refer (quickly!) to your application form, take notes – even hold on to your teddy bear for moral support.
- You don't need to dress up or smarten up. However, you might feel that you want to do this to give yourself moral support.

- You don't need to spend time travelling to interview or wonder if the employer will pay your expenses.

**Disadvantages of telephone interviews (for you)**

- You can't see the interviewer to gauge their response.
- Tension – you never know when an employer might call to interview you.
- They can seem to go very quickly, without giving you much time to think about your answers - so be well prepared!

**The advertisement may ask you to phone the company.**

This gives you total control over the time and place of the interview – although means that you will have to pay for the call. At the time arranged, make sure you are in a quiet location and that you will not be disturbed during the call. Or they may phone you in response to your CV/application form.

You will normally be advised when the telephone call will be made so always be prepared for this:

Keep your mobile with you, charged, topped up and switched on at the appropriate time! Make sure that the reception is OK.

Try and take the phone to as quiet and private a location as possible.

If the call does come unexpectedly and you are not prepared say "*Thank you for calling, do you mind waiting for a minute while I close the door/turn off the radio/take the phone to a quieter room?"* This will give you a little time to compose yourself.

If it really is a bad time, offer to call back, fix a time and stick to it. Check your answerphone message: is it one that you would want a prospective employer to hear? Does it give a professional impression? If not, change it — just in case you do miss a call for any reason.

## Tips

- Keep a copy of your application and information on the company handy, plus a pen and notepad to take notes. Have your laptop turned on if your application is on this.
- Before the call, make a list of your USP's (unique selling points): the things that make you better in some ways than most of the other people who will be applying.
- Don't just read out your notes as this will sound stilted.
- It's useful to have a glass of water to hand during a phone interview (but move the phone away from your mouth when you swallow). You will be doing a lot of talking and you don't want your mouth to dry up at a crucial moment!
- Smile when you dial! (And, more importantly, when you speak): it really does make a difference to your tone of voice.
- Although the interviewer can't see you, you may find it easier to come over in a "professional" manner if you are sitting at a desk or table rather than lounging in bed.

- In a face-to-face interview, you show that you are listening via non-verbal signals such as nodding your head. Over the phone you have to show this by the occasional *"OK", "uh-huh", "I see", "I understand", "yes"* or similar interjections.

- Listen very carefully to the interviewer and try to answer with a lively tone of voice. Speak clearly and not too fast.

- Reflect back what the speaker is saying in other words. This shows you're listening carefully and checks that you are understanding. It is often the most useful way of giving positive feedback to someone: "I hear what you're saying and take it seriously". You can't keep saying "uh-huh" or "yes" for too long without it sounding false.

- Immediately after the interview, write down the questions you were asked and any ways in which you could have improved your responses.

**What questions will I be asked?**

These will be identical to those asked in a face to face interview!

**Will I be given any tests?**

Perhaps – tests can quite easily be administered over the phone. The interviewer may read out a series of statements and you will be asked to say if you agree or disagree. Sometimes this can be done by pressing the telephone keys. The tests involved are more likely to be personality-type questions than reasoning tests. For example, you may be asked to rate the extent to which you felt the following activities reflect your personal style, from 1 (not at all) to 5 (a lot):

- Meeting new people.
- Setting yourself targets to achieve.
- Working on your own.
- Repairing mechanical equipment.

## Video/Zoom interviews

As technology continues to grow, and as virtual work becomes more accepted, Skype interviews become closer to the norm for many industries and roles. A Skype interview requires just as much, if not more, preparation than you'd take on for an in-person interview. Preparation can ensure that you can combat technical issues, know how to appear well on camera and have a successful Skype interview.

## What is Skype?

Skype is a video conferencing program that allows for remote interviews over your computer or phone rather than appearing in-person. You should treat an interview on Skype similarly to one that would normally be face-to-face. Below are tips for a Skype job interview:

- Make sure you have Skype installed.
- Dress professionally.
- Use an appropriate background.

- Face the light.
- Sit at a proper distance.
- Arrange the Skype windows.
- Test your microphone and video.
- Take the interview in a quiet location.
- Log in a little early.
- Show engagement in the conversation.
- Take turns speaking.
- Prepare for the interview.
- Maintain good posture.
- Share your screen.
- Record your interview.

### Make sure you have Skype installed

If you don't use Skype regularly, make sure you have the program installed on your computer ahead of time. Downloading and going through the installation process can take a long time, so you don't want to do this right before your interview and risk showing up late. If you already have Skype installed, make sure it's updated and you have your log-in credentials handy so you don't have to reset your password beforehand.

### Dress professionally

Even though you aren't meeting in-person, you should still dress as if you are. That means appropriate business attire from head to toe, even if the interviewer won't be able to see all your clothing. Look at how your outfit appears on camera, then consider your background and if your outfit of choice contrasts well. Staying in formal attire for a Skype interview will send the message you're very interested in and serious about the role.

## Use an appropriate background

You can choose different backgrounds on Skype, which may be fun for a call with friends, but your best option for an interview is to either blur your background or make sure that what is behind you on video is appropriate. If you're taking the call in your bedroom, make sure your background is free of piles of laundry or an unmade bed. If your office tends to be a catch-all room, organize it before your interview so the only thing your interviewer is seeing behind you is a space that's well put together.

You can play it safe by setting up your desk in front of a solid, clean wall that's free of distractions.

## Face the light

You'll want to be well lit during your interview so your potential new employer can see your facial expressions, engage with you and ensure the call goes smoothly. If you can, set up your computer so you're facing a window that lets in natural light or a desk lamp that will keep your face illuminated. No matter how it's done, it's important for the light source to appear behind your computer and focused on you.

When practicing your interview, take a look at how you appear in your outfit, background and light source of choice to make sure there isn't a distracting glare coming from any part of your setup.

## Sit at a proper distance

During an in-person interview, you wouldn't sit on the opposite side of the room from the hiring manager. You also wouldn't sit uncomfortably close to them. Apply this same rule when on a Skype interview and maintain a proper distance between yourself and your computer camera. When you test your video before entering the call, make sure that your face, shoulders, and upper chest are visible, and that there is space between the top of your head and both sides of your body in the shot. The more centred you are in the frame, the better your distance is.

## Arrange the Skype windows

To make sure you're maintaining eye contact, arrange the video windows within the Skype program appropriately. When you open the software, the window with your hiring manager's video may be off to the side, so drag it over to be as close to the camera as possible. That way, your interviewer is seeing you look right at them and not anywhere else.

## Test your microphone and video

Before your interview, test your microphone and video settings to make sure they work. If you go into the interview with working equipment, you're more likely to send the message that you have adequately prepared yourself for this meeting. Your microphone should transmit your sound static-free and your speakers should work to receive audio from the hiring manager, while your video should be centred and camera clean. To make sure everything is working as it should, visit your Skype settings and perform a test run of your equipment.

### Take the interview in a quiet location

The amount of background noise during your interview can affect how well the call goes, so try to set up your computer in a space with the least amount of potential interruptions. Let those you live with know that you'll be taking an important call and that they shouldn't disturb you if they can help it. If there's a chance that an interruption will occur, such as with kids or dogs, be upfront with the hiring manager right away so they aren't too surprised if it happens. Consider silencing your phone and pausing pop-up notifications on your computer too.

Especially if your new job will require that you take customer or client calls or be a part of a lot of business meetings, your hiring manager may expect that you'll have a space dedicated to performing your work that will allow you to do so professionally. However, if an interruption happens during your interview, acknowledge it while remaining calm and focused on your discussion.

Log in a little early-Just as when you arrive at an in-person interview a couple of minutes early, you should also try to arrive to the Skype interview early. Depending on the Skype settings, you'll either be able to enter the meeting room before the interviewer, in which case they'll see you waiting once they've arrived, or you'll only be able to enter once the host has given you permission. In either case, a hiring manager will see that you are eager to chat about the role and adequately prepared for the interview.

## Show engagement in the conversation

It's common for a hiring manager to rely heavily on body language as an accompaniment to what a potential hire is saying, but Skype interviews aren't exactly the same. Therefore, it's important to work at maintaining an engaging conversation through this platform. This means asking questions, nodding, keeping eye contact, smiling and acknowledging what the other person says.

## Take turns speaking

While it's a great tip to remain conversational over video, you still must exercise some caution to make sure both parties hear each other and you both do not accidentally interrupt what the other is saying.

Even unintentionally interrupting, like to answer the interviewer's question, can momentarily mute one person's microphone so the other can speak, a feature that can ultimately cause confusion and the need to repeat part of the conversation.

## Prepare for the interview

As with any interview, prepare for the role by practicing your answers to popular interview questions, readying your portfolio, making notes of valuable responsibilities or projects that will showcase your experience and looking into the company you're applying with and the role you're interviewing for.

You can also have some questions of your own prepared which shows that you put in the extra effort. Another way to prepare for the interview is by performing a test run with a friend on Skype. This will allow you to test your equipment and get used to speaking to someone over video.

You may also want to read up on how to fix any technical issues and have that information in front of you before starting your interview.

If your audio or video goes out or another common error occurs, you'll be better prepared to fix it quickly and get right back into the discussion.

## Maintain good posture

Good posture showcases your professionalism, especially in this kind of scenario. While taking a seat in your favourite chair can entice you to slouch, be mindful of the posture you're using during the interview. Instead of sliding down in the chair, sit up straight with shoulders back and eyes forward. You may even communicate better and display more confidence with proper posture.

## Share your screen

A significant benefit of a Skype interview is you can showcase your prior work as it relates to the role in a way that an in-person interview may not afford. If you have an online portfolio, ask the hiring manager if you can share your screen so they can see your website, the social media accounts you've managed or sales numbers you have in a spreadsheet. Be prepared with this information in another window so you don't have to spend valuable time searching for it—this will also show that you prepared well for the interview.

## Record your interview

Ask for permission to record the interview. Being able to refer to the interview can help if you expect to have multiple Skype interviews before landing the role. You'll be able to both see how you can improve next time and prepare for the next steps based on information that you and the interviewer discussed.

## Zoom interviews

Zoom is one of the medium used to carry out remote interviews. By now, you've probably heard of Zoom, the video-conferencing software has exploded in popularity since the start of the COVID-19 pandemic. People around the world are using it to stay connected with loved ones, host happy hours with friends, and, yes, even interview for jobs. If you have a job interview coming up on Zoom, you might feel intimidated — especially if you're not very familiar with the platform. Many of the tips relating to Skype are also pertinent to Zoom.

## What is Zoom?

Zoom is an online platform for video and audio-conferencing, much like Skype, Google or even FaceTime. However, Zoom offers a lot more features, and many companies use it to host online meetings, training sessions, seminars, and now video interviews.

## How to get started with Zoom

If you've never used Zoom, getting started is simple:

- Install Zoom on your computer. This takes less than a minute, but you'll want to do this with plenty of time before your interview just in case something goes wrong.

- Open Zoom (this should happen automatically after you've installed it) and click "Join Meeting." There's no need to create an account unless you want to.

- Enter the meeting ID or personal link name, which the company you're interviewing with will provide. It'll likely be an 11-digit number. The company may also send a link over via email, which will bring you directly to the meeting.

- It's best to practice this a few times before your interview, just so you feel comfortable. It won't hurt to ask a friend or family member to hop in a Zoom meeting with you so you can test everything out.

- On the day of your interview, join the meeting a couple of minutes before it officially begins. If the meeting host has not yet started the meeting, don't fret. As soon as the host joins, you'll be able to enter the meeting.

## Preparing for your Zoom video interview

It's important to prepare for your video interview. In many ways, this will be easier than an in-person interview: You don't have to worry about traffic, and, if you're already employed, you won't have to worry about missing a huge amount of work. But there are still things to keep in mind.

## Dress to impress

As we have stressed numerous times in this book, just like an in-person interview, carefully plan what you wear. Wear something polished and professional, but don't fret as much about what you wear from the chest down — you'll be on a video after all.

## Location is key

You'll also need to scout out the perfect interviewing location in your home.

## Have a tech backup plan

Since you're relying on technology — which can be problematic just when you need it most — have your computer plugged in and charging. You'll also need a back-up plan; in case you have issues with your Wi-Fi internet connection. If you have an unlimited plan on your phone, you can connect your computer to its hotspot. Or you can download the Zoom app on your phone and have the meeting there. While this isn't ideal, it should work.

## Make sure you can be seen and heard — and emote

Just like you would for an in-person interview, it's necessary to practice and prepare questions you want to ask — but there are a couple of additional things to keep in mind. First, make sure your audio works and your video camera are clear. If it's not, check out your Zoom settings by clicking the arrow next to "Stop Video." You'll find the audio settings there and can adjust accordingly.

Second, make sure your excitement and personality shows through the computer. This can be more difficult than it would be with an in-person interview, so focus on your body language, eye contact, tone, and energy while you practice. If you want feedback, you can always record yourself and watch it over, or connect with a professional interview coach, who will set up a mock video interview and provide feedback.

## A few simple Zoom interview tips

Zoom has a lot of features, but you won't need to know all of them for your job interview. Instead, focus on these simple hacks (overleaf) to ensure your interview goes as smoothly as possible:

## 1. Use the video preview to your advantage

The nice thing about Zoom is it doesn't throw you into the video conference when you first join. Instead, it will show you a video preview. Use this as an opportunity to make sure your camera is smudge-free and perfectly positioned.

## 2. Touch up your appearance

Not many people *love* staring at themselves in a camera but Zoom has a feature that'll make you feel a little bit more polished. When you're in the video, click the arrow next to "Start Video" and go to settings. There, under the video tab, check the box that reads "Touch up my appearance." This adds a subtle filter to your screen that smooths out your appearance, toning down any splotches or blemishes you might be worried about.

## 3. Resist adding a virtual background

By now, you've probably seen all the creative backgrounds people have added to their Zoom meetings — from the set of "The Office" to Disney World to even outer space. Zoom basically turns your background into a green screen and lays an image over it.

Although you might be tempted, it's best to not use this feature during a video interview. You'll want to stay as professional as possible, and the focus should be on you and the interviewer — not whatever's in the background. If your background is incredibly cluttered and you have no other option, look for a simple Zoom background, like a classic bookcase or a tidy office. If you plan to use this feature, make sure you create a Zoom account and enable the virtual background set-up on your profile. Practice with it so you know it'll look good.

### 4. Utilize full-screen mode

Eliminate any potential distractions on your computer by closing any other tabs and making your Zoom window full screen with the "maximize" button on the top right side of your screen. This is a super simple move, but it'll help you stay focused throughout your interview.

### 5. Choose your favourite layout

There are a few options for how you view your screen when using Zoom. Determine which layout you prefer from the following:

- **Active speaker:** This will enlarge the video window of the person who is talking. So, if the interviewer is speaking, their video will take up most of your screen. If a second attendee is also on the video, then their screen will stay smaller until they begin speaking.
- **Gallery view:** If you want everyone to be the same size, including yourself, choose gallery view. This will show all the meeting participants in a grid view. This makes it easy to view everyone at the same time.

To change your layout, select the option you want in the top right corner of your screen.

## 6. Know where your "mute" button is — just in case

In case of an emergency, you will want to know that your "mute" button is in the bottom left corner of your Zoom window. Because you're interviewing at home, keep the mute button handy just in case the dog starts barking, the kids start screaming, or the fire alarm starts ringing.

The mute button is also a great way to help eliminate any background noise on your end while the interviewer is talking, especially if you live in a big city or on a busy street where sirens are commonplace.

Of course, in an ideal world, your Zoom job interviews will go flawlessly and be distraction free, but while everyone is at home during COVID-19, there are no guarantees. Just make sure you know how to properly use Zoom and do your best — Interviewers understand this is an unusual time for everyone.

## Robotic interviews!

A few companies are now using virtual interviewers using life-like avatars to ask the questions normally asked by an interviewer via online video interview software. It helps companies to save money and improves the candidate's interview experience. The average cost per hire in the UK is about £5,000, and this software may save 43% of the screening cost by reducing the time involved in the process.

The avatar keeps interviewees engaged via visual, audio and text prompts and is visible during the whole process so that the interviewee has something to focus on. Avatars are consistent, asking each question in the same way to each interviewee.

Now read the main points from Chapter 8 overleaf.

****

## Main points from Chapter 8

How to Perform Well in Telephone, Skype and Zoom Interviews.

- Phone interviews are real interviews held over the phone rather than face-to-face.
- You are more likely to have a telephone interview with one of the large corporate recruiters than with a small or medium sized company.
- Phone interviews vary in length from 20 minutes to 1 hour, with the average length being half an hour:
- Skype/Zoom Interviews are becoming as widely used as telephone interviews, they are particularly helpful for international recruitment when interviewing the candidate in another country – e.g. for TEFL teachers and are particularly relevant in the time of the pandemic.
- A Skype/Zoom interview/will be more like a real-life interview than a telephone interview.
- The use of recorded video interviews is increasing. These started with technology companies, but have now spread to mainstream employers

*Now turn to the conclusion.*

# Conclusion

## Bringing it all together.

It is now time to recap on the most important points raised in this book. There are certain main points that you must remember prior to attending that all-important interview.

## Planning

We discussed planning earlier. In order to make sure that you give the best interview possible you need to ensure that you have planned everything in advance. Get familiar with the job, with the company and what they do. The internet can be a useful tool here. It is vitally important that you are thoroughly conversant with the company. Analyse the job specification and description and make sure that you have an in-depth knowledge of what is required from the successful candidate and that you are able to convince the interviewers that you are the person for the job.

Make sure that you have your application form with you at the interview and that you can cover all your periods of employment including the gaps.

## Preparation

You need to ensure that you are thoroughly prepared for the interview. Ensure that you know where the organisation is and if necessary, do a dummy run to their offices to ensure that you understand the journey and any difficulties involved.

Make sure that you are smart. This goes without saying. Carry out your own private rehearsal answering questions (see chapter on interview questions) out aloud in order to build your confidence. If a presentation is involved then rehearse the presentation thoroughly make sure that you have absorbed the hints in the chapter on presentations. This is most important.

When you are at the interview relax, appear confident. Remember that although it is an interview, and you will understandably feel nervous, if you have prepared thoroughly and are confident there is no reason why you shouldn't get the job.

**Feedback**

If for some reason you don't get the job, make sure that you ask the interviewers for feedback. The reasons that they give for not offering you the job could be useful in future interviews.

Good luck!

****

## Other sources of help and assistance

### Jobcentre plus

Jobcentre plus offers training, help and job search resources when a person is out of work. See www.jobcentreplus.gov.uk.

### Learn Direct

Learn Direct has a government funded help line available to everyone. By ringing the freephone number you will get advice about local sources of help on career and learning issues. See www.learndirect.co.uk for more details.

### Internet sites generally

There are numerous internet sites around that can give assistance with interview techniques. Many are displaying job vacancies. Job seekers can access these pages free of charge. Listed below are a few of these sites.

www.prospects.ac.uk This is the UK's official graduate careers website, provided by Graduate Prospects, part of the Higher Education Careers Service. It is aimed primarily at graduates.

www.reed.co.uk. This site is owned by Reed Employment. It is a comprehensive site, as befits a large recruitment agency and there are many useful tips for those putting together a CV and also for those seeking to enhance their interview skills.

www.fish4.co.uk. This is a large commercial site with job adverts direct from employers, also including interview tips.

www.freelancer.com online recruitment agency finds freelance work.

https://www.indeed.co.uk Job Search by Indeed. A main online job site in the UK. Search millions of jobs from thousands of job boards, newspapers, classifieds, and company websites on indeed.co.uk

The main newspapers, the Guardian, Times, independent etc all have their own recruitment websites which might be worth a visit.

In addition to the above, there are many more online recruitment sites advertising job vacancies.

****

# Index

****

## Appendix 1

## Sample CV's

If you intend to send out your CV to prospective employers you will need to ensure that it is well laid out and clear. Overleaf are examples of two different layout styles of a CV. The information is the same and includes all elements. However, you should include and exclude information depending on the perceived requirements of the employer. For example, it may not be necessary to include religion or location or other facts. This depends entirely on the employer.

****

## Example 1

**PERSONAL DETAILS**

| | |
|---|---|
| Full Name: | Barry Hargreaves |
| Occupation: | Computer Analyst |
| Address: | 37 Meridian way Kingston Surrey |
| Telephone Number: | 1234 6789 |
| Date of Birth: | (optional) |
| Place of Birth: | Rich Street Ninetown Anywhere |
| Nationality: | British |
| Religion: | Buddhist |
| Marital Status: | Married |
| Next of Kin: | Mrs Hargreaves address as above |
| National ins no: | 10987654321 |
| Driving License: | Current full |
| Health: | Excellent |
| Preferred location: | Anywhere at all |

---

**Education, Training and Qualifications**

Education:  1990 - 1997

Northampton Grammar School

GCSE Passes:

| | |
|---|---|
| English | Grade  (d) |
| Biology | (c) |
| French | (c) |
| Physics | (b) |
| Economics | (b) |

## Higher Education

1997 - 2000  Faversham Polytechnic, High Street,

Faversham Northampton

BA   Computer Sciences: Pass with distinction

Year One:       Computer Theory

Year Two        Advanced Computer Theory

"               Computer Trainee on placement,

                ElectronicsSystems Ltd,

                Long Road, Northampton.

                Assisting the Chief Engineer

                developing computer systems

Year Three:  Applied Computing

---

## Short Courses

Short course computers Limited July 2004 Fault finding on Computers (2days)

September 2004        Software Analysis (1 week)

December  2005        Advanced Spreadsheets (1 week)

---

## Professional Association

Royal Institute of Computers

Fellow of the Institute October 2006

## CAREER HISTORY

April 2015 - current.

Authentic Computers, Northampton. Consultant

In this post, I am acting in the capacity of consultant to the private and public sectors, advising on systems usage. I am employing the technical know-how gained in my previous jobs.

I am conversant with most computer packages
Salary: £25,000 Per Annum

February 2010 - April 2015
London Borough of Shepwhich. Senior Computer Manager

In this post, I had responsibility for overseeing a change in the authority's computer system. This involved carrying out systems analysis and producing a brief for the council, who subsequently accepted the brief and instructed the computer department to effect the change.

After two years I was promoted from Computer Manager to Senior Computer Manager.

Jan 2006 – Feb 2010
Wing Computers Limited, North Circular Road, Northampton
Whilst employed by Wing I obtained the status of Fellow of the Royal Institute of Computer Scientists. My main duties for the company were to oversee the development of a computer system for a local authority. This involved giving technical advice to the authority and supervising a workforce of 23 people who

were directly involved in the installation of the equipment. During this time, I gained experience of the following packages: Wing 1 - Wing 2 - Super Wing-Wing for Windows

November 2000 - Dec 2006

Barnard Computers Limited, Northampton

Whilst in this post, I commenced my professional Institute Exams. My main duties were to assist the Deputy Chief Executive in developing a new operations system.

---

**Personal Interests**

I am interested in squash, badminton and indoor football. In addition, I am interested in studying history and Science. I enjoy walking in the countryside and swimming. I also like to participate in the community and am on the local conservation committee. I speak French and German fluently and have traveled to these countries for my current employer on business.

---

**Health**

Excellent

---

**Preferred location**

London

---

**Example 2**

| | |
|---|---|
| Name | Barry Hargreaves |
| Address | 37 Meridian Way Kingston Surrey |
| Telephone number | 020 8 123 6789 |
| Occupation | Computer Analyst |

---

**Career**

**April 2010 - current.**

Authentic Computers, Northampton. Consultant

In this post, I am acting in the capacity of consultant to the private and public sectors, advising on systems usage. I am employing the technical know how gained in my previous jobs.

I am conversant with most computer packages

Salary: £25,000 Per Annum

**February 2010 - 2015**

London Borough of Shepwhich. Senior Computer Manager

In this post, I had responsibility for overseeing a change in the authority's computer system. This involved carrying out systems analysis and producing a brief for the council, who subsequently accepted the brief and instructed the computer department to effect the change.

After two years I was promoted from Computer Manager to Senior Computer Manager.

**Jan 2006 - February 2010**

Wing Computers Limited, North Circular Road, Northampton

Whilst employed by Wing I obtained the status of Fellow of the Royal Institute of Computer Scientists. My main duties for the company were to oversee the development of a computer system for a local authority. This involved giving technical advice to the authority and supervising a workforce of 23 people who were directly involved in the installation of the equipment. During this time, I gained experience of the following packages:

Wing 1 - Wing 2 - Super Wing-Wing for Windows

**November 2000 - Dec 2006**
Barnard Computers Limited, Northampton

Whilst in this post, I commenced my professional Institute Exams. My main duties were to assist the Deputy Chief Executive in developing a new operations system.

---

**Professional Qualifications**
Fellow of the Royal Institute of Computer Scientists, 2006.

---

**Education, Training and Qualifications**
Education: 1990 - 1997
Northampton Grammar School

GCE Passes:

English          Grade (d)

Biology          (c)

French                    (c)

Physics                   (b)

Economics               (b)

## Higher Education

1997 – 2000 Faversham Polytechnic, High Street, Faversham Northampton

BA   Computer Sciences: Pass with distinction

Year One: Computer Theory

Year Two: Advanced Computer Theory

Computer Trainee on placement,

Electronics Systems Ltd, Long Road, Northampton. Assisting the Chief Engineer developing computer systems

Year Three:  Applied Computing

## Short Courses

Authentic Electronics Limited

July 2004 Fault finding on Computers  (2 days)

September 2004      Software Analysis (1 week)

December 2006    Advanced Spreadsheets (1 week)

## Personal Interests

I am interested in squash, badminton and indoor football. In addition, I am interested in studying history and Science. I enjoy walking in the countryside and swimming. I also like to participate in the community and am on the local conservation committee.

I speak French and German fluently and have traveled to these countries for my current employer on business.

Other personal details

| | |
|---|---|
| Date of Birth: | (optional) |
| Place of Birth: | Rich Street Ninetown Anywhere |
| Nationality: | British |
| Religion: | Buddhist |
| Marital Status: | Married |
| Next of Kin: | Mrs. Hargreaves address as above |
| National ins no: | 123456789 |
| Driving License: | Current full |
| Passport Number: | 456789 |
| Health: | Excellent |
| Preferred location: | Anywhere at all |

****

The above two examples represent two different ways of laying out a CV. The information is the same but is presented in a different way. The reader will see different facts first. You must decide which will be of primary importance for this particular employer. The key point is that you are presenting what you consider to be the most important and relevant facts first.

Example one concentrated on personal details first, followed by education and career. Example two placed immediate emphasis on career then education, with personal details last.

**Different CV's**

**School leavers**

Most school leavers will have very little experience of the job market, with the exception of a Saturday job or evening employment. The fact that you do not have a career history to demonstrate should enable you to keep this part of your CV brief. Generally, you should aim to keep to one side of A4 paper.

Your education will be the most important part of your CV if you are a school leaver. You should try to include any work experience that you may have had. This will include work experience programs and Youth Training Programs.

You should list all work experience, highlighting grades achieved. If they are not too good, you should omit them. The employer can ask for details if these are needed. You will invariably have to explain the nature of the qualifications. If you are older then the school system will have changed.

You should attempt to make a connection between your hobbies and your personal qualities, which show your skills and aptitudes. Organizational skills are generally valued and participation in voluntary work can help to create a positive image of you as a person. Do try to avoid quoting too many interests or give the impression of being a flighty person. The employer is usually more concerned that you are able to settle into a work environment, especially as you have not experienced the world of work and the attendant discipline. If you have been involved in the arena of student politics, be careful how you mention this. Some employers are not over-keen to employ someone who they perceive may cause disruption or upset a well-established applecart. There is no harm mentioning areas of responsibility such as president of your branch of the National Union of Students, but don't go much beyond this, unless of course a prospective employer knows you and your political skills and history are an asset.

## Long Term Unemployed

If you have never been employed, or it has been many years since you were in employment, the main problem that you will find is explaining the gap in your employment, and demonstrating that you are still employable. At all costs you must avoid giving the prospective employer the impression that you feel hard done by or have a chip on your shoulder.

Employers want to take on cheerful employees, not those disgruntled and harboring past resentments. At the end of the day, you have a selling job to do and it will be no easy task to convince the employer that you are ready to re-enter the world of work.

## Redundancy

If you have been made redundant, try to show that you understand the company's reasons behind the re-organization. If the organization went out of business, try to show that your attitude towards this was responsible. And do not let the reader of the CV think that this was in any way due to you.

Show that you have somehow learned from the experience by doing something positive which will help you in your future career. If you have undertaken formal training to prepare for a career change or advancement, be specific in how that training fits the job applied for in the new company. If you are circulating many unsolicited applications, you must still tailor these to the organizations and the kinds of jobs that you are interested in. Your application is wasted without this.

In unsolicited applications, ask if they have any current vacancies for the sort of post that you are seeking. Ask whether their future planning indicates that there may be vacancies available in the near future. Remember to include your most positive points, including the ability to work immediately. This can be a very valuable plus-point in your application.

**Career Breaks**

If you have had a career break to raise a family, for example, or are changing career direction it can be very difficult to convince a prospective employer that you are serious about the post and are committed to it. You must convince the employer that you are firmly committed to working and that you have a real interest in their field of work. Cite any refresher courses that you any have taken and emphasize that your childcare arrangements are adequate.

Your career change may be due to circumstances beyond your control. If you have undertaken retraining, sound positive about this and indicate that it was thorough and that you took it seriously. If you are returning to work after a spell in prison, note the Rehabilitation of Offenders Act 1974. This covers people with certain past convictions, but who have not been convicted again for specific lengths of time. After these trouble free periods, the individuals are deemed to have spent their convictions and do not have to declare them.

If the conviction has no bearing on your prospective employment and you can avoid mentioning it you should do so. However, you must not lie about it and may have to declare it if asked.

If you are returning to employment in the United Kingdom after working abroad, you must show how the position you held abroad was similar to the kind of job that you had here. The recruiter must be convinced that the change in culture would not mean that your training and abilities have a completely different slant. You may be able to stress the positive side of this too, emphasizing your increased awareness of the international business scene. If you have worked overseas, references may be difficult for the employer to follow up. Testimonials, translated as necessary, may be useful in this situation.

\*\*\*\*

## Appendix 2

### Ideal Covering letters

A covering letter with your CV is really a letter of introduction and is usually the first thing that a prospective employer reads. You should always send a covering letter with a CV or application form. If your application is speculative this is even more important.

The reason for sending the letter is to make sure that the prospective employer has all the facts. Make sure that you keep a copy of what you send.

### Rules of letter writing

Ensure that you use a good quality paper, ideally A4 so that it fits well with other documentation. Do not use colored paper with elaborate designs. Most employers cannot stand this approach. Your letter can be typed or handwritten as long as the end result is that it is legible. If a person cannot read your letter then they will dispose of it, along with your CV. If you know that your handwriting is bad then type the letter. Use black ink for writing or typing letters as this makes it easier for photocopying. The usual rules of spelling and grammar apply in letters as they do in the CV. The overall effect has to convince the reader that they are dealing with a professional.

Any letter that you send must be formal. It must be well set out and show respect to the person that you are writing to. Remember, if you start the letter by saying 'Dear Sir' you must end by saying 'yours faithfully' and that if you use the persons name you must end with 'yours sincerely'. Note that the 'f' and the 's' are in the lower case.

Note how the title of the recipient is given in the advert. If the text asks you to reply to a specific person then you should do just that. Always address the person by their surname and never their forename.

Put your address in the top right hand corner of the letter. You should not put your own name here but leave it until the end of the letter, where you will print and sign. You can, if necessary, put your telephone number under your address. If you put the name and address of the recipient, this should be further down the page on the left hand side. Depending on your style of letter, this date can either be beneath your own address or under the recipients address.

Space the letter out as well as you can. Again, the main rule of letter writing is that the recipient has to get a clear impression of the writer. The more legible the letter, the better laid out, the better the impression. If the letter is short, such as a letter requesting an application form then you should start further down the page. If there is lots of information in the letter, then you should commence higher up the page. If you can possibly fit it all on one side, then all the better.

Overleaf you will see an example of a letter forwarding a CV to a prospective employer. Following this, you will see a further two examples. The first one is requesting an application form.

The second is returning an application form to a prospective employer.

*Example 1*

Daniel Green                              37 Meridian Way
Raft Enterprises                          Kingston
Codley Way                                Surrey
Northampton                               Tel: 020 8 123 6789
N1 F45

1st October any date

Dear Mr. Green
Your Ref: ABCDEFG. Vacancy for a Computer Scientist.
I would like to apply for the position of computer scientist with your company. I saw the advertisement in the Times 9th March 2023.

As you will see from my enclosed CV, I have been a computer manager since I graduated from Northampton University in 2003. I have been involved in the public and private sectors, overseeing systems analysis and installation. I believe that I have the experience that you are seeking and would be very interested in working for Raft Enterprises.

I look forward to hearing from you.

Yours sincerely

Barry Hargreaves

Example 2

37 Meridian Way
Kingston
Surrey

John Baldrick                    Tel: 0208 123 6789
Baldrick Enterprises
Jones Street
Northamption
N1 4RG

1st October any date.

Dear Mr. Baldrick
Your ref: COMP 123. Computer Manager

I am responding to your advertisement in the Times newspaper for a computer scientist. Could you please forward me an application form.

I look forward to hearing from you.

Yours sincerely

Barry Hargreaves

Example 3

37 Meridian Way
Kingston
Surrey
020 8 123 6789

Mr. J Baldrick
Baldrick Enterprises
Jones Street
Northampton
N1 4RG

5th October any date

Dear Mr Baldrick

Please find enclosed my application form for the post of computer manager advertised recently in the Times Newspaper.

I look forward to hearing from you soon.

Yours sincerely

Barry Hargreaves

## Letters to agencies/consultants

Again, when writing to agencies and consultants, employ exactly the same rules of letter writing but be more specific about what you want if you are writing general letters, not in response to a specific advertisement.

You may wish to give the consultant more information so that he/she can suggest vacancies that you may be interested in applying for. You need to convince the consultant that you are proficient in your chosen field. Therefore, your application must look professional. Remember that it will go from the consultant to a number of companies.

The golden rule when letter writing is that a letter must be laid out on quality paper, well written, clear and to the point.

## Appendix 3

### Tips on emails to prospective employers

### Job application emails

As with business emails, it is now common to email companies with CV's, job applications and cover letters.

Your covering email is quite important as this is quite often the first thing that a prospective employer might see. First impressions can be lasting impressions!

### Subject line

After you have checked that you have the right email address, you need to make sure that you put the right information in the subject line. This immediately shows the respondent what the email is about and ensures that it does not get overlooked or counted as spam.

### Addressing the email

In the same way as a covering letter, a covering email should be addressed to the right person as outlined on the job specification. Be sure to address the recipient in the correct manner, either as 'Mr' or 'Mrs' or 'Ms' (if you are not sure of status). If the job specification simply states 'S. Wilson' then just addressing it as S Wilson can be quite insulting if you get it wrong.

If you are applying for a job that requires an initial covering letter then it is a good idea to keep your email short and to the point. One paragraph is enough which should act as an introduction to you as a person, what you can bring to the company in question and why you are applying for the position.

## Attachments

If you need to attach your CV and covering letter to your email, there are a few things that you need to be wary about. Firstly, make sure that your documents are named correctly.-simply calling your CV 'CV' isn't very descriptive, especially when your potential employer is likely to be drowning in them. Make sure you include your name when naming your documents and be sure to actually attach them to your email before sending. Its surprising how many people forget!

When signing off your email, you should try to end with something positive and polite like; "Thank you for taking the time to review my application. I look forward to hearing from you". This will show that you are enthusiastic and polite, two attributes that all employers want to see.

Also be sure to sign off with "Kind Regards" or "Yours Sincerely" rather than something chatty or informal.

Taking time over your email should help you in your quest for a job. First impressions, lasting impressions!

****

**Appendix 4**

**A few tips on application forms**

If you are applying for a job that requires you to fill in an application form, there are several important rules to remember. When you receive the form, never fill in the original in the first instance. You might make a mistake and not be happy with what you have written and might need to start again. By then, if you are using the original, then it is too late. Always copy the form and fill it in with a pencil. This way, you will not suffer if you make a mistake.

Application forms can either be written or typed. It is up to you to exercise your discretion at this point. However, only if your handwriting is neat should you fill in the form by hand. A typewritten form will be more immediately readable and make a better first impression. Send the application form in with a brief covering letter. Do not falsify the application form, as this will form part of your contract of employment when offered the post.

The job application should be treated much the same way as your CV. As was mentioned earlier, when you interpret the job advertisement you need to analyze the nature of the job before compiling the CV. You should do exactly the same with an application form. The first task is to read the job description that should normally accompany the application form.

It is absolutely essential that you understand the requirements of the post. Many organizations will send a person specification outlining the essential and desirable criteria, which the applicant must meet before he or she is considered for the post. Although the essential criteria are the most important, if those short listing for the post have a number of good candidates then they will revert to the desirable criteria as a way of further eliminating candidates.

It follows that, when completing an application form which has a person specification with it, then you should fill in the application carefully following the requirements of the post, ensuring that you meet the essential and desirable criteria. In addition to essential and desirable criteria, there will be a skills required section, which will generally outline the skills and abilities, which the person must demonstrate. Make sure that when you fill in your application form that you follow the person specification closely, you have read and understood the job description and that you comply with all the requirements. If you do not, then you are wasting your time.

Normally, there is a space on an application form which asks you to outline your experience to date and to demonstrate why you want the job. You should be concise and to the point. On too many application forms, applicants really go to town in this section, producing a whole life history amounting to many sides of paper. This is totally unnecessary and will, more often that not, result in your application being thrown in the bin. You should follow carefully the requirements of the post, from the person specification to the job description, and lay out clearly and concisely your experience to date. You should then relate this to the job on offer and explain why you think that you are the ideal candidate.

If there is no job description or person specification to work from, then you will need to read very carefully the requirements of the post from the advertisement, and then construct what you think are the main aspects of the job related to your own experience. In this way, you can present the interviewer with a picture of yourself. It is not very often these days that an application form is not accompanied by a job description.

If you feel that you are on uncertain ground, for example when faced with filling in an application form without a job description or person specification, then you might want to contact the company concerned and request further information.

## Content of application forms

The application form will proceed on a logical progressive basis, much as a CV is compiled. The form will start by asking you your name and address, some will ask your date of birth. The type of organization that you are applying to will very much determine the application you are being asked to fill in.

Some application forms are designed with great care and reflect the ethos of the organization, such as omitting to ask certain information on an equal opportunities ground. For example, some organizations deliberately do not ask for information relating to age as this is thought to affect the perceptions of those who are short listing for the post. As has

140

been mentioned it is now mandatory for all organizations to ignore age when considering an applicant for a post.

There will be a space for a phone number. This is important, as the company may want to contact you by phone shortly after the interview to discuss the possibilities of offering you a job.

Other details at the beginning of an application form might be sex, marital status and country and place of birth. This again will vary depending on the organization you are applying to.

The next section of the form will ask you for details of education. You should start with your most recent job first. However, it is very important to read the application form as it might state otherwise.

Applications might ask for salary information and reasons for leaving the post. As discussed, on a CV it is not wise to volunteer this information, with the exception of final salary. However, some application forms may require this and will say so.

If the state of your health has not involved disability but has involved long periods off work then you should try to demonstrate to your employer that this problem is now in the past and that this will not affect your future employment.

Most applications end by asking for references. These will normally be from your current employer and one other, such as someone who has known you for a long time. If you are not currently employed then the reference should be from your ex-employer. Make sure that you know what your employer or ex-employer is going to say about you in advance. It follows that you should let this person know that you are going to use them as a reference.

Many employers do not bother taking up references despite asking for them. Others always take them up as a matter of course. Some applications state that they will take up references when a candidate is short-listed. You should contact the company and state that you do not want this as it could affect your relationship with your employer (if this is the case).

If you have not yet been employed then you should use school or academic references. A second reference might be a personal reference. Some applications will ask specifically for a personal reference. In this case, it is better to use a professional reference, i.e. someone with whom you have worked in a voluntary capacity or even someone you have worked in a paid capacity for.

There are a number of other questions that may appear on an application form, such as whether or not you have a driving license or whether you speak any other languages. Notice periods, possible start dates and periods of notice, plus membership of professional bodies may also appear.

There may also be a requirement to outline your ambitions. Be careful and tailor this to your employer's requirements.

****